Painting South Pier

Dawn Hogue

Water's Edge Press

Sheboygan, Wisconsin

Copyright © 2019 by Dawn Hogue

All rights reserved. This book or any portion thereof
may not be reproduced or used in any manner whatsoever
without the express written permission of the publisher
except for the use of brief quotations in a book review.

Printed in the United States of America

ISBN: 978-0-9992194-6-1

Water's Edge Press
Sheboygan, WI

waters-edge-press.com

Also by Dawn Hogue

A Hollow Bone

Contents

Spring

First Signs 9
Predators 10
Crocus 11
Solitude 12
Surely Not Now 13
The Color of Water 14
Persistence 15
Russula Crenulata 16
May Day 17
They Shoot Rockets From South Pier 18
Migrants 19

Summer

Painting South Pier 23
Sailor 24
Power Struggle 25
Red Shoes 26
Buoyancy 28
Crane Dance 30
Aeolus Sleeps 31
South Pier Aesthetic 32
So Much for a Heat Advisory 33

Fall

Blue Harbor 37
Fishing 38
Color Wheel 39
Gone to Pot 40
September's Revenge 42
Notice 44

Winter

First Snow	47
Keeping Warm	48
Glow	49
Mad Dogs	50
Horizon	51
Winter Business	52
Transience	53
Skipping Ice	54

Acknowledgements

From Everywhere a Little: A Migration Anthology: "Persistence"
Inscape Magazine: "Russula Crenulata"
Stoneboat Literary Journal: "Crane Dance"
Van Gogh Dreams: "Aeolus Sleeps"
Verse Virtual: "Solitude," "The Color of Water," and "May Day"

About South Pier

The South Pier District in Sheboygan, Wisconsin is a 42-acre peninsula at the convergence of the Sheboygan River and Lake Michigan. Once owned by C. Reiss Coal Company, the property was used to store coal, salt, fertilizer, and petroleum. The area is now a vibrant shoreline community that welcomes tourists year-round.

First Signs

The river has thawed, even upstream
where for weeks thick ice stubbornly
refused to move.

The mergansers are still afloat, though
they will probably head north in a week
or two, and I have heard from a friend
that the pelicans are on their way.

A pair of mallards has come ashore,
waddled across the busy street to
look at the property between our
apartment building and the next.

The wheat-dry grass seemed suitable,
but in the end they chose the lot
across the street for their nest.

I admire their wisdom. Before long,
leaf blowers and lawn mowers will
disturb everyone's peace.

And just yesterday a pair of pale red
house finches rested in the spindly limbs
of the young maple outside our window.
They perched at ease, no March winds
blowing under their feathers.

I have yet to see a robin, but hope has
arrived full-color even without his
orange sign.

Predators

South of South Pier a tiny swath
of sand is strewn with driftwood. Spring's
jagged ice-floes tore low lying limbs from
the river bank and dragged them into the harbor.
Debarked limbs lie scattered now, thrust upon riprap
or resting on the beach.

One is a thousand-pound crocodile, its head raised,
alert to nearby birds. But dunlins and sanderlings
who trot on new-washed sand have nothing
to fear as they peck for morsel bits.

Crocus

What courage it takes to be a crocus,
pushing its outstretched arm-like leaves
through snow-chilled soil, then blooming—
yellow or purple—shouting life in spring's cold sun.

Solitude

Captain Joe—or so they call him down at the pub—
knows it's his long, white beard that children
stare at, gape-mouthed, long after Christmas
is over, wondering could it really be?

But at 80 Joe has let go of the joy he once
found in such ponderings. He now seeks peace in
solitude, the easy oneness with water. This serene
spring morning he pilots his boat along the shoreline,
towing a bright blue rowboat, a delivery
to a woman who lives up river
in a small, red house.

The woman simply likes to row, she has told him,
up and down the river, shade or sun, sometimes
out into the harbor on calmer days. Later, from
her memory, she will write about birds
and the color of water.

He guides the rowboat near her dock where she
waits. He watches her secure the boat—bow and
stern—with swift and perfect cleat hitches.
Job done, he waves to her and thinks with a sigh:
*Now this is the kind of woman I would have married,
if that day had ever come.*

But—No regrets. He's too old to regret anything,
especially today as he navigates the river passage
back to open water where south winds have freshened.
Nothing he cannot handle. He thinks with a deep, inner
pride of the many white caps and black squalls his
Lady of the Lake has survived.

She has weathered with time, like he has. But today
they reach through April's cats paws as if they were
new off the launch.

Surely Not Now

It can't snow now
not after the street cleaner
has swept away salt grit and winter dirt
not after the first piers are back at work
in the river ready for boaters and anglers
not now that the first of many collector plates
blue on the back bumpers of well-tended cars
has begun the ceaseless parade down South Pier Drive
not now that robins have returned to sprouts of green grass
and fat red buds and blue flag iris

surely not after all of this
could nature be so cruel

The Color of Water

My father had a cabin on a root beer lake,
water colored by tannins from pine forests
of the Mesabi Range in far-north Minnesota.
Bloom Lake was only a hiccup in the ice-age
scrape that left deeper, wider sand-lined lakes,
fished first by the Ojibwe and the Fond du Lac,
later by my grandparents and parents, lakes
named Winnibigoshish and Kabetogama,
vast and blue under clear cobalt skies.

Today is a slate blue day yearning for the sun,
and I am far from Minnesota memories, years
removed from iron ore lakes and spike-pine
forests, walleye and black bear and our little
muck-bottomed lake, filled with
the sediment of history.

I walk the shore of this water now,
and despite clouds, the sky is clear and bright.
It is the lucent color of water that lights the morning.
Lake Michigan is glazed celadon, pale jade.
Its white-crested waves roll to shore in
ancient cadence, language of all water.

Persistence

In the dune sand atop a high shelf
of Lake Michgan's Sheboygan shoreline,
a scraggly juniper has crept about,
this way and that, looking for a foothold—
a thing I take for granted. Even my dog,
who has paused here to let the breeze
blow back her ears, who raises her muzzle to sniff,
finding a wisp of fish, the linger of last night,
pads her way over the golden ground without
taking a moment to consider every little stretch
the plant has made to sculpt itself even this far.
Not able to do more than set the shallowest
of roots, it nevertheless remains alive. When
now and then vicious winds have attacked
with scraping sand, it has persisted, webbing
its winding, barky roots upon inhospitable earth.

Russula Crenulata

Nearly a week of rain
has given life to spores
settled in the spring soil,
and this morning's early light
reveals a mushroom, bright white
against the lawn's green edge.
Genus Russula is most common,
though I would not tell her that,
the little slight-stemmed lady
in her Elizabethan collar
cupping the morning dew
in her upturned cap.
Her visit will be
brief enough.

May Day

The only ribbons around which we dance today
are streams of rain from rooflines that target our feet.
On shiny splashed sidewalks we dash from door to door,
lift umbrella arms over our heads, and swing and swerve
away from puddles. Inside we shake as dogs, flicking off
the showers of April that refuse to relent.

Even the daffodils bow down under the weight of water,
despite their bold yellow flounces, skirts of gold,
demure in a May Day mist.

They Shoot Rockets From South Pier

Hope plumes over the lake. Eager
students on shore watch their
invention soar.

The sky accepts what it cannot
know—for the moment only—
as matter will not hold,

unless it reach beyond gravity,
but even then, orbital pull will
reign. Freedom is illusion.

Migrants

a black flock flies west,
steers along the river, we
see them only once

Painting South Pier

Mother Nature colors this morning hazy-blue.
After broad strokes across open fields, she swishes
her sepia-loaded brush into clear water upstream.
Now she watches the river take her muddy tint
eastward to the harbor.

She lifts her brush to paint a small red boat rocking
upon a rose-brown ribbon streaking an ever-burly
lake. On the pier, Prussian Blue-shirted men wait
with silent poles, while upon southern beaches
foam-white rolls come to shore.

On a small yellow beach, she dabs two families
who make the most of the last week before school.
She dots the beach with blue umbrellas and rainbow-
striped towels before she sends her children out
to wade in sand-filled waves.

A thunderous storm warns from the west. Dipping
into deep Cadet Blue, she presents the lake itself
as mighty, beginning to churn and growl, hurling
regurgitated algae upon riprap, Hooker's Green
splashes breaking bright upon the stone.

Later, sirens wail and she anticipates the wild, pelting rain,
knowing she will plunge into black to darken the rising swell
of clouds as the afternoon sky turns to night. In an instant,
she knows she will draw her knife across Barite White
and scrape a lightning strike.

Violently unwrapping new canvases, she will paint
the roaring gale that will tear down trees and wires.
As she renders a perfect mess of land and water, she
will scrub Van Gogh swirls and smile at the memory,
how she'd given him the idea to paint the wind.

Sailor

A solitary cormorant
floats and bobs
on the river,
its DeLorean
wings raised
for balance
or breeze,
and the day
finally gentler,
cooler, not
like those before
that sullied me
with sweat heat,
humid, hair-frizzing
dew points, and I want
to join him as he sails
lightly on the water,
orange beak lifted,
steel eyes staring
up at the sky, perhaps
wondering how long
to stay, perhaps simply
for the pleasure of being

Power Struggle

The starched-stiff flag at the mini golf
bleats and wails as it fights to remain
tethered to its halyard.

In the east, the dawn is outmatched.
She has given up and let go of gauzy pink
remnants that disappear into weakening blue.

The west wind is angry, with something to prove.
He drags behind him a battalion of black clouds,
clones of Cerberus, snarling their intent.

At the shore, the complicit lake lifts her fists and
surges against the riprap, growling so loud
she drowns out even the wind.

Red Shoes

It won't be until later that they notice.
Mother will ask, "where are your shoes?"
The boy will respond only with a quizzical
expression—he has no idea what she means.

"My shoes?" he thinks.

I could answer, but I am not there.

I imagine them—the boy's family—having arrived
late in the afternoon at their suburban Chicago home,
tired and sunburned after a week's stay at Blue Harbor.
They clamor out of their van, dragging from vacation
unwieldy suitcases, bags of musty beach towels, and
coolers of soda cans and half-eaten leftovers
floating in icy water.

Father hoists a sky-blue kayak over garage rafters.
After work tomorrow, he will take the van to the car wash.
The boy's twin sisters twitter and sneer at their mother
who tells them in tired tones to drop their suitcases
near the laundry room. She knows she won't get more
out of her pre-teens than that.

The boy, sand still between his eight-year-old toes,
squints to gather his memory. He thinks of how they'd
walked back from the South Pier ice cream parlor for
one last swim in Lake Michigan, one last free moment,
how his fingers, sticky with chocolate and sprinkles,
had come clean in the lake, how he'd wandered into the water,
farther than his mother liked. Her warning to stay close
had died in its fight with the seagull's song. Alone, shoulders
bare in the late August sun, he'd stood, feet wide apart,
and swirled his hands in the blue green sparkle. Then, even after
his father had called him in, the boy had arched back upon
the surface and let himself float, eyes closed tight against the sun,
closed tight against the fact he'd soon be strapped into the car,
highway miles humming beneath his feet.

She'll say it again. "Yes. Your shoes. Where are they?"

He will search. He will shrug.

They will all search.

Weeks after, as he sits restlessly in his desk, watching
dry erase markers play out in spelling and math on glossy
white boards, his toes confined in new shoes, longing for
sand and summer, I notice from a distance, a bright red blur
in late morning sun, a curious spot of color distinct from sand
and tall, pale grass. Up close, a monarch is also deceived.
It flits above, lights on a winding lace, stays for a moment,
resting its wings, open, then shut, then flutters up and away.

Buoyancy

The first time I saw the ocean I was
eleven. My parents' divorce the year
before had left me alone. We drove east
so my grandmother could visit her sister.
My mother was at the wheel.

I sat behind her—my nine-year-old
sister got the other window,
and our younger brother stayed
trapped between us through
endless miles.

The women in the front seat
rarely concerned themselves
with us—except to tell us to stop
fighting or to look out the window
to see what we were missing.

As they smoked cigarette after cigarette,
my mother listened to her mother's stories—
growing up on the farm with her sister,
their nine other siblings. Being poor never
meant sad. They were always laughing.

We had left the flat Midwest one morning
in a rusty Rambler and days later we stood
on a long, white beach, our rubbery road-legs
aching, and we looked out at the ocean
at colors we had never seen.

Go on, get your feet wet, she must have
said, my mother who had brought us there.
We did not have much, but this cost her little.
This was something she could give us—
something she could give her mother.

I was eleven when I first waded into
an ocean, unafraid. I dove, plunging
my head under, turning onto my back.
It surprised me at once, how easily
I floated. Not at all like the clear,

chlorine pools where I had learned to swim,
there always a conscious act of floating,
here floating as if part of me, the way
my arms are part of me, the way
my thoughts are.

Years later I learned about salt water
and buoyancy. That summer, I discovered
for the first time my own weightlessness,
my own oneness. My ears submerged,
I could silence the world.

Long after we stuffed ourselves
back into the car, I would close my
eyes and conjure the blues of that
cloudless sky, the white sand, the sun
bleaching everything it touched.

I have Lake Michigan now, a block from
where I live. This inland ocean, colors akin
to my memory, Atlantic-like waves crashing
into shore, splashing an aging concrete pier.

I have aged, too. I no longer float on water,
though as I watch summer children wade
out and lie upon their backs, I sometimes
feel an urge to join them, and wonder if out
upon those lake waves I might feel eleven
all over again.

Crane Dance

You're not a shore bird who dives for fish.
You're at home in marshes, new-plowed
fields, expanses of land with a view of
a long, pink sky. You hunt for mice, voles,
easy-to-snatch grasshoppers in late August.
I've seen you on my country drives in your
long-legged stance, out past the farmer's
snow fence, hunting, dancing—so free.
In the air, you fly near the others, but
are never constrained by geometry.
Instead you move at will, on a current
or whimsically through a cloudy strand—
move as the moment dictates.
I am more self-conscious.
Even when music compels me,
I dare not dance, dare not listen
when my heart screams
"go wild."

Aeolus Sleeps

inspired by The Starry Night, Vincent Van Gogh

Aeolus sighs and exhales,
almost ready to surrender
to stillness who will rule
until his return. Winking
at the setting sun,
he gathers its warmth
and blows a gentle gale
into the sky, where it gathers
stars and clouds and dusk,
and rolls them into a noisy ball
that knocks its din into hillsides
onto rooftops, shakes canopies
of trees and pricks itself
upon the steeple before
settling, undisturbed,
into the corners of the
night, finally to sleep.

South Pier Aesthetic

It's July and even with threat of rain, kayaks
skim the river. We have passed the solstice and
understand it's now or never for our summer.

Morning is most sublime early, when like us,
the sun needs another hour to fully climb from sleep.
Afternoons are lazy, and the dog curls in elusive shade.

Japanese lilacs have burst into showy perfume and we
had better like their scent. Or go with the monarchs, who
prefer to dance in floral linden, making milkweed jealous.

By evening, we venture toward the lake to hear her sway,
back and forth, shore to distant shore, a Zen-like quiet,
where even high waves, storm-less, calm us.

The high moon sometimes fights the fog, but never
for long. Weather changes moment to moment, wind
rocking like wave rocking. July lulling us to sleep.

So Much for a Heat Advisory

The weather service has drawn
a red outline—jagged geometry
on the map. It zig-zags the shoreline,
crosses counties, and boxes us
in an urgent notice to take care.

But they generalize and forget
we have our own weather here
on South Pier so close to the lake.
Drive even a few blocks west and
you'll be sweating for a cool breeze,
while we might shiver and clutch
a sweater closer.

Not that we're complaining.
Step by step out on the pier, we can
leave the worst of summer behind.
The lake breeze is breath itself.

We advise you to join us.
Remove your shoes and walk the sand.
Let the lake lap your toes. Or slowly
wander the dune path, where
the soft, misty horizon
will settle you.

Fall

Blue Harbor

Approach from the west,
idle at the crest of Pennsylvania Avenue
and watch two blues come together at rest
in the horizon near the harbor shore—
steel blue, bright and clean,
teal blue, soft, and deep.

A ribbon of sand-brown separates them,
the demarcation from a shift in weather,
winds from the east swirling now
from the north. The sky is light, pastel,
interrupted only by one thin white stripe,
thin clouds arch over tall masts, sails furled.

Fishing

The crew works on cleaning now, readying their fleet
of fishing boats for winter storage. They work leisurely
at mundane tasks: rubbing dead insects and their frass
from fiberglass until it gleams, power-washing the decks.
They seem in good spirits for being land-locked, but
why not? They've been blessed with a sunny day, mild
and calm. Or have they chosen it? The boss in his email:
better get this over with. He stands on the river walk—
arms folded over his chest—watching, waiting.

We have watched the boats all summer, heading out
to the harbor, crew on board, anxious anglers hoping to lure
a photo-worthy salmon or lake trout. The captains blast
the horn before they make no wake downriver.

I envy the view they will have once they clear the harbor—
endless sky and open water. The sounds, too, the lake lapping
against their hull. Gulls' cry. Back on land they'll weigh
their catch, gut and fillet, then haul out the hoses to rinse
clean, flushing away blood and bits.

All of that is done now.

Tonight the sky will pink and turn black long before dinner.
In the dark, lights will gleam and sparkle on the water.
Saturday morning South Pier will crowd with lawn chairs
and hopeful poles of those who gather every chance.
But too soon the river will freeze. First a thin glaze,
then ice so thick only those most hearty will venture
out to auger holes and drop their lines.

When we will all wait—
in the long dark.

Color Wheel

Bright white siding
rust red roofs arch up
into blue sky, white-clouds
to the north, white masted
boats bob in deep blue water
emerald-headed ducks sun
on bleached-brown river piers

In October maple leaves burn red
against white and lavender powder-puffs
tinged at the edges by the yellow sun
they work to keep hidden

Green grass grows as if it knows
how soon the snow will fall

Gone to Pot

"Then goeth a part of ye little flocke to pot, and the rest scatter."

--from William Tindale's "An answere vnto Sir Thomas Mores dialoge," 1530, in which the old phrase is used to mean 'going to the cooking pot', or being chopped up and cooked for food.

That old phrase, something gone to pot,
in one sense, what's useable for food
added to the stew, let the rest go as nature
will have it—to roam or to seed—seems

fitting when I consider the large stucco-
sided planters set at intervals near South Pier
sidewalks. They rise like curved, copper stew pots
simmering as if on Tindale's iron stove grates.

Volunteers came mid June, brought flats of annuals,
maybe leftovers from picked-over garden centers,
donated for just this purpose—cosmos, zinnias,
marigolds, red byzantine salvia—

all set carefully into churned up soil,
then left to rain for water. Their roots
took hold despite a hot spell of weather,
and soon color crept above the pots'

burnished edges. From my balcony view
I am glad for the flowers. In downsizing
I have given up my own gardens and I
miss the prospect of their summer show.

I suppose I thought I might adopt these
container beds, as consolation, so on my daily
walks I sought to ferret out and remove offending
weeds. But soon, I had to concede to being

outmatched by chickweed, for one, whose
hair-tangle roots resisted my yank, or spurge
or speedwell, gone one day, then back, it seemed,
the next. My intentions, well and good, were futile.

I realized even my small gain against horseweed,
a much less tenacious foe, was nothing in the wider
war. So, resigned to defeat, I let the weeds take
over, my attitude toward them mollified

by the fact that they had as much right to be here
—even more since they had planted
themselves, traveled by bird or breeze—
as these coddled hybrid plants we prize.

It's mid-September now. Black nightshade
berries, tomato's tiny purple sisters, shine
in sun and shadow. Plump-fingered children
won't be poisoned if they steal one. It's true

many of these intruders are edible, could be
eaten outright or snipped—root, leaf, or flower—
and put into soup for health or as a cure for what
ails us. In our ignorance we frown and pluck

out clover, mallow, plantain, and pigweed.
We see as ugly the rusty-seeded spires of curly
dock that crown over tiny yellow marigolds
that bloom shyly, bereft of strong sun.

Only the deep red cannas maintain their realm.
Weak jesters like shepherd's purse who fight for
an audience at canna's roots are kept away by a guard
of deep green soldiers, arms reaching to the sky.

Soon the snow will put us all to rest, and flower-pots,
empty and dormant, will cease to concern me. I will
write about sleet storms or ice floes or wonder how the
ducks fare, while in the earth little seeds lie in wait.

September's Revenge

Standing before red and orange TV maps,
weather watchers bark in surprise that
temperatures are "not normal" for this time
of year and warn of storms. But September
knows better. As August's closest sister—
it's been said they could be twins—
she is often hot. Still, people do go on
about her, always expecting her to be
mild-mannered, respectful of her place.
It isn't like she went completely mad.
She brought mid-eighties, thought they
might appreciate the gesture, now that
their stores are stocked with pumpkins
and mums. It's not as if she hazed over
blue skies or buckled pavement. Kids still
played on soccer fields. Dogs still pulled
on leashes. Anglers still fished.

Don't they see October, her fickle brother,
hiding around the corner, darting his teasing
tongue. "Can't get me," he will say before he
runs. But she will catch him. She always does.
Oh, he can be a gentleman—bow and bring
many a tender evening—but he might as quickly
bring snow, just for spite, just to show he can.
And don't even talk to her about November.
He likes to pretend—now and then—
he can be summer, too, even after he's forced
all the leaves off the trees and frosted morning
windows. He often boasts that he can open
a day as warm as she can. Though he's mostly
bluster. Gray-skied November is probably jealous.
Most of his days are gloomy and he knows it.

September admits to feeling envious herself.
Not of her brothers, never of her cold, damp spring
sisters, no matter how lovely their early flowers,
but of December, her snow sister, the eldest
and most beautiful of them all. December with
her dark and starry skies, her quiet, short days
poets notice.

December hushes the world in gentle snow
and sends it early to sleep. People look forward
to her sister. They set out strings of twinkling
lights that set off her twilight evenings
like jewels. September doesn't begrudge her sister
fame or beauty. She is simply tired of being taken
for granted. After all, September thinks, "I am
the first one who remembers each year to paint the trees."
"Well fine," she grumbles, "Since you didn't like
my yesterday—." I will grant your wishes for a cooler day.
After devising her plan, she calms the breeze, then rests.
Before sleep, she clears the sky to reveal every planet
and star, white against the night.

After a brief, pink dawn, she's ready. September drags
her most somber clouds from the back of her closet
and spreads them out evenly. Then she exhales
a long northern breath. Maybe tomorrow she will
add rain, but today, she wants only to make her point.
Mid morning she watches a green-eyed woman come
out on her balcony to follow a tug as it pushes a loaded barge
up the river. The woman looks off to the ever-darkening
west and shivers, then heads inside to pull on a sweater.
On the lake path, a silver-haired man walks a large white dog.
Waves crash, splashing spray against gray riprap.
September laughs as she blows off his hood, sending him
hurrying home where he will consider the irony
of his desire to turn on the heat.

Notice

It is mid October
and the cold has taken me
by surprise. When I return
home I must remember
to unpack gloves and hats.

One lone fisherman casts
his line from the pier this
morning. I hope his bravery
pays off. Summer, I have
to admit finally, is gone.

At the mouth of the harbor
I turn south on the lake
path and notice at once
the air is warmer, rising
from the water.

I take the boardwalk that
arcs close to shore, walk over
sand-covered slats through tall,
thinning grass and pause on
the crest of the highest dune.

The family is back again,
on the beach just south
of Blue Harbor. They come
nearly every Saturday—for
the kids, I suppose.

A dark-haired toddler grasps
her mother's hand, tugs for attention.
The mother looks at her phone.
An older brother squats and peers
at the sand, draws with a stick,

while his father, yards away,
gazes into the lake sky, gray-blue
today, soft slate, the slightest hint
a weak sun may escape the clouds
for a moment.

First Snow

The first snow came in October,
in ice balls that a north wind pelted
against us, we so unprepared
for weather this brutal, this fast.

On the soccer field, our grand-
daughter's fingers burned bright red
as she watched for the ball, readying
for a kick that never came.

Only a week earlier, we had sat
on the deck in sweaters to watch
another October sunset, bright pink
and orange, navy blue dusk.

We remarked how lovely the evening was,
early street lights gleaming on the dark
river. Indoors, we flipped on the lights
at five. Pitch black by then.

We are never ready.

Keeping Warm

The worst of winter is yet to come
but already I need to bolster myself
with fleece-lined hat and mittens,
a scarf that wraps my neck and face.

Though she is more resilient against
cold than I am, even the dog has her coat,
a rather stylish little thing, quilted in black,
lined in leopard print.

We don our layers and head out,
for I will not give in to the urge
to slink under blankets and forget
the colors of the horizon.

Today the lake is calm, steely
blue against a matching sky.
Two ducks float upon waves
propelled by a reluctant sigh.

We barely see the ebony kitten,
curled on the still-green grass, last
week's snow all but gone. I pause
and take his picture. He sees us,

but doesn't move, doesn't mew.
The dog ignores him, but I begin
to worry. How will he fare when
true cold comes? Is he alone?

Or does he live nearby in a colony?
Maybe they sent him out for food.
A nest of rabbits? A litter of mice?
Or maybe someone left open a door.

Once he makes his way back, they'll scowl
and let him in, wondering where he's been.
And he will find his sunny perch at a south-
facing window, and lick his sandy paws.

Glow

Somewhere they must be stored
most of the year, stacked high
in a warehouse, these wirey green
bristle wreaths adorned with red bows,
red and gold-glittered balls

Until November, when city crews
reach in and grab them by twos
and threes, carry them to trucks,
tossing them in heaps, careful enough
not to break blue lights

Not waiting until Thanksgiving
to turn them on, they glow earlier
and earlier each night, a dim
blue reminder, gentle light
in the dark

Mad Dogs

That old phrase about who goes out in the noonday sun—
What about those who brave the north wind's gale that shoves
the surf onto the pier in plumes of bursting powder? Even
protected harbor waves arch high over the breakwater,
recede, then arch again, and again.

My dog is not mad but maybe I am. Despite fleece-lined hat
and double mittens, the wind still bites my eyes and blurs
my vision so much I wonder if what I see before me is mirage.
Are there *people* out there? Or perhaps just blackened
driftwood bobbing on persistent waves?

I walk closer, blink to clear my sight, and focus— two silhouettes
in black wetsuits sit on surfboards. Out loud I wonder *are they mad?*
December or not, calendars don't dictate everything. Or Mondays
either, I guess. I imagine the early phone call, agreeing to skip work
for the perfect barreling surf, "A Frames" on Lake Michigan.

Horizon

At the blue horizon, pink streaks the earth's arc
creating a dividing line between all I can see
and all I cannot.

Winter Business

A pair of Common Merganser ducks arrived today.
They skimmed the river just upstream from a thin
ice floe, their bright orange feet making a swish-smooth
landing. A small flock of Canada Geese nearer the harbor
has taken no notice of the newcomers.

While her mate dives for a mid-morning snack,
the tufted-headed hen bobs nearby until it's her turn
to hunt for fish, mollusks, or invertebrate tidbits below
the river's rippled blue surface. She and I wait patiently
for his return. Then in an instant she is gone.

The ducks have come to winter here, where we also tend
to winter business—Christmas and a new year to ring in.
Like them, we must brave the weather, though our journey
to find food takes us quickly across town where packages
bedazzle us from supermarket shelves. And most nights—

a movie on TV—we will huddle under blankets until spring,
when we might venture out to our porch on a sunny afternoon.
By then the mergansers will have flown north, perhaps to a
bright Alaskan shore, where they will dive in colder waters
and wait in their high cliff nest for chicks to hatch.

Transience

The river has a landscape too,
like its shore, like its sloping banks.
In fall it presents itself as dark
and foreboding, when the sun
on its axis denies water the
strength of summer light.

In winter the river carries itself as it
always does to the lake, but yesterday,
at the end of December's darkest day,
the river wore an ermine coat, pure
white, glistening. By morning, a
blue sky burned bright.

Today the melting river has become art,
sculpted with snowy ice bricks and translucent
flagstones chipped loose up river. They float
toward open water, unaware it will swallow
and end them. For now, they squeak, competing
for the lead, shard edges clashing.

My attention is drawn to a queen-sized
sheet of ice nearby, an elegant raft of glass,
a motion canvas. Black water gently surges
over uneven edges, again and again, ripples
tapering to the middle, ending
in a frozen glaze.

Skipping Ice

From a distance it appears they walk
on water, biblical proof of God. Knowing
the truth doesn't diminish the effort
my brain needs to adjust to
the dissonant image.

Boys they are, really, these seven
Coast Guard men, out on the river
in their safety regalia, bright orange
vests, rubber suits, braced for winter
water under the ice.

This morning they will practice rescue
drills, each in turn playing the part
of a struggling victim, though
there is no struggle about
who will go next.

I think of kindergarten.
It's the boys whose hands shoot
up "me, me!" before they even
know what the teacher wants,
eager to be heard.

But first the crew must break through,
create an artificial weakness in the thick
January ice, so they stomp, again and again,
until at last one plunges through. To wild
cheers another follows, just because.

Only one of the crew seems disengaged.
Picking up cubes of ice, shattered debris
from the first break through the ice
he sends them up river, where they
bounce and skip like stones.

www.ingramcontent.com/pod-product-compliance
Lightning Source LLC
Chambersburg PA
CBHW020431010526
44118CB00010B/531